One, Two, Three, Four

Lada Kratky

Illustrated by John Sandford

®HAMPTON-BROWN BOOKS

MANY CULTURES, MANY LANGUAGES…MANY POSSIBILITIES!™

One, two, three, four.
A cat with a dish
came through the door.

One, two, three, four.
A hen with dessert
came through the door.

3

One, two, three, four.
A squirrel with pancakes
came through the door.

One, two, three, four.
A mouse with a ham
came through the door.

One, two, three, four.
A turtle with lettuce
came through the door.

One, two, three, four.
A donkey with bread sticks
came through the door.

One, two, three, four.
Let's have a party
and sing this song
once more.